EXECUTIVE ASSISTANT'S GUIDE WITH SOUL AND FAITH

CAREER CONFESSIONS OF A WIFE, MOTHER, DAUGHTER, SISTER AND FRIEND

@Copyright 2018

ISBN: 9781983055614
Imprint: Independently published

Volume #1 Collection
Author: Amal Candido

Website: MyEABlog.com
Facebook: www.facebook.com/myEAblog/
Twitter: @myEAblogdotcom
Instagram: @myEABlog

DEDICATION

To My Mom. You've inspired me so much. Your resilience and perseverance in the face of pain, struggle and uncertainty is unbounded. Your humility in all you have accomplished to provide for your children is a testament to love. I only wish I could do half of what you've done in your life to even come close to be the great woman that you are!

To My Son. Nicholas, you have no idea how much you make me so proud to be your mom. Every day I spend with you is always the best day ever! You've taught me all about Transformers, Pokémon and Yokai Watch. Nothing in life is as rewarding as watching and being a part of you growing up. You are my heart, my light and my love!

To My Husband. How many relationships work so well when one has fallen, the other is always there to give comfort and support. It's not great timing how that worked out. It's knowing when to stop and make the other a priority until we are both back on solid ground together. Agape Love at its finest!

INTRODUCTION

Let me start first by saying, I am not a therapist or a doctor, or hold any degrees in advising anyone how to run their lives. I have enough on the go juggling my family life, work life and all the demands that those put on me!

You will read chapters that I have experienced and lived through. Some good times and tough times. Life is just full of hidden surprises here and there, where sometimes you will stop and think to yourself I was lucky with this or wow I had gone through hell and back! One thing I know for sure every challenge I faced, help me to grow in faith and tested my strength level each time. It created in me a strong resiliency and survival mode whenever it was needed.

I've been working for years, through high school and beyond. I've also lived as a stay at home mom until it was time to put away the small toys and living behind the toddler world. Who knew that I would face biases of my own returning to the workforce after 7 years, trying to convince people that I have great skills and I would like to put them to good use. It took a bit but perseverance won and I was ready to make the leap back in! To work with real adults and talk to these same real adults using real adult words! Now my work-life balance life begins...or so I thought.

Now you see, I've always had an issue with separating the work-life balance "thing" when it comes to the bigger picture. You work because you have to and you live a life at home because you want to. It's the splitting of these that I am not convinced can be done 100%, because I believe we all bring our whole self to work whether we like to admit it or not.

What I am saying is that you need certain things from home to make your day at work easier to manage. Specifically, I'm talking about three fundamental things, Faith, Mindfulness and Self-Reflection.

Faith at work will give you the strength you need to move your day forward and deal with obstacles that get in the way, one way or another, over time.

Mindfulness will give you the clarity to see things as they are, on the inside and outside of yourself. This clarity will help clear out the clutter and the noise around you and help you grow to be the person you were meant to be!

Self-Reflection is key to living a fulfilled life as it takes your mind off comparing your life with others around you. It will bring you to focus on your 'self' to be able to answer key questions along your journey such as; Am I on the right path? Who do I want to be? What do I want to do? Where do I need to go?

What I know for sure; as much as I hate pain and fear, they both played a big role in my journey personally and professionally. I have not mastered courage, endurance or faith completely, but I am happy to say it's a work-in-progress daily for me. So much so, to the point I began to wonder if God is intentionally putting me through the valleys to learn and master my beliefs in Faith, Mindfulness and Self-Reflection, in order to be who He wants me to be!

To that end our God is an intentional God after all.

With Love,

Amal Candido

TABLE OF CONTENTS

CHAPTER 1

CAREER CONFESSIONS OF A WIFE, MOTHER, DAUGHTER, SISTER AND FRIEND

CHAPTER 2

PAYING IT FORWARD - GIVING IS GREAT

CHAPTER 3

APPRECIATION - SHARING YOURSELF FROM THE HEART

CHAPTER 4

THE GIFT OF GIVING WHEN YOU LEAST EXPECT IT

CHAPTER 5
TRANSPARENCY - DON'T MAKE IT PERSONAL AND YOU WILL THRIVE

CHAPTER 6
MOVING BEYOND DISCOURAGEMENT - UPLIFTING YOURSELF SPIRITUALLY @WORK

CHAPTER 7
BODY AND SPIRIT WELLNESS - CONSIDER IT AN 'ANYTIME' SPRING CLEANING

CHAPTER 8
THE ROOKIE EA - THOUGHTS AND TIPS TO MAKE IT THROUGH THE DAY

CHAPTER 9
THREE CORE LEADERSHIP QUALITIES NEEDED
TO MAKE A POSITIVE CHANGE

CHAPTER 10

BETTER @HOME AND @WORK SERIES

BETTER @HOME AND @WORK
HELPING THE MIND AND BODY

BETTER @HOME AND @WORK
5 WAYS TO GET YOU STARTED ON BOOSTING
YOUR SELF-CONFIDENCE

BETTER @HOME AND @WORK
THE IMPORTANCE OF PROFESSIONAL GROWTH
THROUGH PERSONAL READING

BETTER @HOME AND @WORK
HOW TO DEAL WITH THAT INNER STRUGGLE OF
SELF-DOUBT

CHAPTER 11
FEAR AND EMOTIONAL PAIN THAT
COMES WITH CHANGE

CHAPTER 12
WHAT HAVE YOU DONE TO HELP
OTHERS IN NEED?

Chapter One

CAREER CONFESSIONS OF A WIFE, MOTHER, DAUGHTER, SISTER AND FRIEND

So some of you might wonder why I picked that tag line for my first book. Well I have decided on the tagline of "career confessions of wife, mother, daughter, sister and friend!" for so many reasons that covers a personal & professional level. I just couldn't choose between one or the others....Because I am all those EVERYDAY of my life.

To raise a son and love him deeply

I was a daughter, a sister and a friend to many before I began my journey as a wife then a very lucky mother. There is something to be said about being a mother that is so rewarding!

I am a mother to a wonderful, intelligent 12-year-old son who during his early childhood years, taught me so much more about myself and how to love deeply and grow as a parent. He is a gifted child with all the quirks and challenges that comes with being gifted.

The thing is, I have spent most of my time raising my son before I started to consider a career as an Executive Assistant.

Traveling was my life until my favorite little bundle of joy arrived!

Before I got married and had a child of my own, I was all about traveling. I had gained my experience between education and working in various verticals within the Travel & Tourism industry.

All that came to a stop when I got married and a year and half later pregnant. Traveling continued but with a purpose as we moved to different countries in the first few years of marriage.

Without any immediate family to lend support, I chose then to focus all my energy to raising my son. Motherhood was the trend and now my new gig!

I am grateful for the choices I have made.

I am grateful that things have worked out this way, it helped me focus on Nicholas. I am positive it would have taken far too long to find out that my son is gifted and would require a lot of attention and help to navigate through how to be "his normal".

Anyhow, the point that am trying to convey is; I spent most of my life in a supporting role thinking of others in a nurturing way, emotionally, financially if I could, be there for my family and friends provide encouragement when needed, words of wisdom, sounding board and soft place for my family and friends to land on.

My heart is full of love to share, that I am most happy when am supporting, giving and putting a smile on someone else other than my own self. So, the idea of a career never really crossed my mind, as much as of the idea of enjoying second pay-check.

I wanted to contribute now financially with my husband and at same time I knew I needed to create a person with a new identity.

My contributions and accomplishments would not just be as a wife & mother but also as a career-oriented woman! Could I do it all? Would I want to? I am a Libra and of course the Libra in me must do things equally, otherwise there is no joy in life.

So, this book is going to cover all sorts of aspects of life, my hope is that it will be relevant to whomever wishes to read it, whatever stage of life they are in and perhaps, share their experience with all of us.

Live Love Laugh

Chapter Two

PAYING IT FORWARD

I still had not met her in person, nor could I pick her out of a crowd.

I met this young woman when I started as a rookie EA (executive assistant). I was new to the role and so eager to make connections with fellow EAs like myself. God forbid I thought, that am at the same level as those seasoned EAs. I did not realize that I needed to put in the endless years of experience, before I could count myself an excellent EA or worthy of a similar title.

Anyway, this young woman, was so kind to me over the phone. I still had not met her in person, nor could I pick her out of a crowd. What I did know for sure was that she was soft spoken, had sweet voice and while humble, she had this aura of kindness about her that I sensed every time we spoke! She would calmly answer my questions with patience and her words chosen so carefully, were gracious.

One time on our phone conversation to book a couple meetings, I said to her "You know I am new at this and you have been so nice and helpful. We really should meet face to face." So, she laughed and said "That's true Amal! We should meet, since we talk to each other almost daily. We could at least put a face to the name." So, we planned on a date & time and agreed to meet.

I'm going to fast forward now...right to the part we met and created a bond...

Though I am trying to make this story short, I can see that I'm not very good at writing short stories! So I will do something now I NEVER do with my friends. I'm going to fast forward...right to the part we met and created a bond that started first as colleagues at work and grew into this wonderful cherished friendship.

The thing is, this young woman has seen me through all sorts of challenges at work at the time when I was a newbie. She helped introduce me to the right people to make my life easy at work and joy of joys, she took the same commuter train as I did. While on the train, she took every opportunity to extend her friendship circle with me. She believed in paying it forward and just her luck, I was ripe to receive positive payment of any kind! I was in the middle of a change within my department and was lost as to what that change is going to look like.

Whether it will be a positive or negative change we spent so much time talking about different scenarios. Her advice at the time was "hang in there you are a good person Amal; if you move on and support another executive, this may be good for you. You never know until you try it and if you don't like it, I will help you find another role".

...she has never forgotten the promise she made to God and herself to "pay it forward".

So fast forward again (you're welcome), I did go with the new change however it was something I did not choose but was rather forced upon me. Working as an EA can be quite the challenge when "the fit" or chemistry between the executive and the EA is not there. Tension and irritation over small annoyances are magnified tenfold and can be difficult to navigate on a daily basis. I had tried in many ways to make it work, but it just didn't seem the right fit. My new friend and I had discussed plans on looking for other roles internally and she would ask around for me.

Having known me for a relatively short time, she stuck her neck out for me and recommended me to an EA that was retiring and asked her to meet with me and interview me for her role.

"Why are you helping me? You have been kind and patient and honestly, I don't understand why?" She told me that in the past someone did a good deed for her and she has never forgotten the promise she made to God and herself to "pay it forward". Now was that time, she felt, about using that opportunity with me.

She must have known inside that I would honor and choose to pay it forward when I am able to someone who needs it. Honestly, she shocked me because I was not used to meeting people that live their life as such in a work environment of all places. For me this was a profound experience on so many levels; from friendships to building and cultivating those relationships at work that they stay with you forever.

Paying it forward is about
- helping someone opening doors for others when needed, anywhere on a professional or personal level there are no limits!

- Sharing your wisdom on anything from leadership, to vulnerability, to calendar management, tasks that can make life easy on the job or tips & tricks on how to use power point presentations

- Helping a rookie in the role on do's & don'ts

- Sharing your best practices
- How to command a conference call with 20 other EAs that are senior than you.
- How to navigate work politics, cultures, and teams.
- How to network and use those connections for the greater good.
- How to build a strong network of EAs, to draw upon each other as a resource for best practice or mentoring
- Be gracious (in giving) with your time
- Using the simple act of a small gesture... for some it hits "the feels" bigger than the grand ones.

...it is kindness? Leading an ear? A soft place to vent? Be a trusted source of comfort.

So if you have an opportunity to pay it forward to a fellow EA, think of what you can do to make another fellow EA's life easy; it is kindness? Leading an ear? A soft place to vent? Be a trusted source of comfort.

I have met many wonderful EAs over the years, and I am blessed & grateful to each of them. Their valuable advice and acceptance of my rookie ways, helping me to grow professionally and building those relationships beyond work. I thank them all for their support, and encouragement they have given me, cheering me on my successes and for being there to catch me when I fall, supporting me, free from judgment.

Chapter Three

APPRECIATION - SHARING YOURSELF FROM THE HEART

This topic is very close to me and carries so much baggage on a personal and professional level. Maybe the reason I have come to put so much value on appreciation started since childhood. We all want to feel appreciated and valued for our contributions whether professionally or personally. Often the foundation of this value begins in our early years.

For me, I truly believe what Dr. Brene Brown wrote in her book 'Gift of Imperfections', "in absence of love and belonging there is always hurt". This started for me, alongside many others, with the feeling as a child of never quite being good enough, smart enough, obedient enough, pretty enough, etc. I can honestly say this feeling transitioned into my growth from childhood to adulthood as it has for many others.

Through all the accomplishments I have achieved to help and support others in succeeding in their roles there was always this nagging feeling that something is missing.

As I continued building my career as an executive assistant, the one thing I discovered was a looming feeling of never quite being enough for my bosses, coworkers, and team members that I'd supported through each role. Each department I moved on to within the same organization, through all the accomplishments I have achieved to help and support others in succeeding in their roles there was always this nagging feeling that "something is missing".

The more I produced and provided great work the more people took, I thought that will be appreciated but unfortunately it was never really the case! All it did was continue the cycle of feeling undervalued & appreciated for work submitted.

Frequently, when no one remembers to put a deposit in your "I appreciate you bank account", it creates feelings of resentment or negativity towards the work that you are passionate about.

As if the lights turned off or went out of from deep within, these are not easy feelings to shake when your accomplishments are not acknowledged, much less celebrated.

The questions companies and managers should be asking themselves everyday is "have we appreciated our employees or team members today?"

If you want to foster an environment that celebrates, grows, fails or succeeds all together, it all starts with Appreciation.

My favorite quotation from Albert Schweitzer "Sometimes our light goes out but is blown again into flame by an encounter with another human being. Each of us owes the deepest thanks to those who have rekindled this inner light."

"I've made a decision to move to a new organization recently, leaving the place where my career as an EA began."

To share a recent short story; I have made a decision to move to a new organization recently, away from my current one that I have invested time in and where my career as an EA began.

This was not an easy decision for me in so many levels. I knew it had to be done for a bigger plan in the future that I may not be able to see right now. I must trust and hope it's a change for the better. With mixed emotion I chose a leap of faith and to dare greatly, to make a change that will impact me professionally and personally.

I have had the fortune of speaking with many EA's so far in my career. The reality of feeling valued for their contribution boiled down to the following questions asked of themselves.

- Do you need to continue to feel undervalued for the work you do?

- Do you want to work for an organization that does not see an Executive Assistant role as a business partner and contributor of the organization?

- Do you want to be in an environment that fosters true collaboration and teamwork? Or pretend it's there?

These questions have helped to support my decision in taking a leap of faith! Change is not easy and having the guts to move forward for a new chapter, rebuilding a new story requires strength and resiliency. My personal past experiences have taught me to see God's timing as opportunities for his soft and safe landing for me!

"I started to say my farewell to colleagues and team members..."

In the past week as I started to say my farewell to colleagues and team members, as is almost always the case, a few will stand out as genuinely expressing appreciation. There it was the appreciation given for which I am truly grateful to receive. It is good to know what I do everyday as a professional, made a positive impact to someone's life. A sense of having fulfilled accomplishments set in.

Looking back to the transition, I think of a quote from Mother Teresa that sums up the way I choose to live my life: "Be kind and merciful. Let no one ever come to you without coming away better and happier." That, to me, is the gift of appreciation!

On a personal note, I have found the simple truths of appreciation are:

- Everyone wants and needs it
- It doesn't have to be something big
- Appreciation is a free gift that you can give to anyone you encounter- it is completely your choice.
- Make it personal
- Be creative
- Surprise people if you can

- Be sincere
- Have a plan
- Share yourself from the heart
- Make it memorable
- You will receive more than you give

The one I live by everyday and I enjoy the most is Share myself from the heart.

To me, this is about always bringing my authentic whole self to every situation with actions, words and passion, with the intention of bringing joy to someone else who needs it the most.

Chapter Four

THE GIFT OF GIVING WHEN YOU LEAST EXPECT IT.

By her giving, I received the gift of appreciation.

What have you done to ease the pain of others lately?
This blog is close to my heart and is special because of the kindness shown to me by a few women that I worked with! They made me believe in human kindness, that it still exists out in the world we live in and at work in the least of all places I expected to see it. I made a promise not to reveal their identity, but I wanted to share and honor their act of kindness. I will talk about them all in a future blog, so stay tuned for stories around some amazing women that I honor.

Below is my gratitude to one of these women.

It was on a rough day at work and this one young woman, who likes to stop by for a quick chat here and there, were talking. We were randomly chatting about silly topics and catching up when she noticed I was tearing up! "Amal, you are not yourself today what's bothering you?" was all it took for her to ask the one question that had me break into tears.

...it is going to be near impossible for me to move up to be the breadwinner from my status right now as I am barely a large muffin winner.

Against my normal instincts to keep my private life private, I started to tell her about my dilemma. I was going through this challenging journey and I was not sure how I will manage.

My husband had lost his job, my mother was diagnosed with breast cancer and was scheduled for surgery & treatment right away. (I will dive into that topic in a later blog dedicated to Mother's Day).

I have to admit my mother's diagnosis was my worst nightmare at the time, among other ones including possibly losing my home.

So, given where we work, she gave me ideas on mortgage payment options when under financial stress, also asked what my husband does so she can pass his resume on to friends. It was this point in a surprise that she opened about her own cancer journey.

We both ended up crying now. She felt my pain and how much I had to carry on my shoulders. We were talking about options and sources of income that could help my situation. We laughed at the same time knowing that it is going to be near impossible for me to move up to be the bread winner from my status right now as I am barley a large muffin winner.

We were interrupted given this conversation had taken place at my desk. That concluded the extent of our chat for now.
Do you know what this young woman did next? This is what I want you, who are reading this to focus on; the act of kindness and the gift of giving when you least expect it from strangers.

As I sat at my desk during lunch time she came back to hand me an envelope. At first, I was a bit confused but that fell away quickly to welling tears again as I opened the card inside.

With sweet yet simple words, 'have a Merry Christmas to you and your family' and a $100 bill attached, the look in my face, frozen with words I could not speak, and my heart now suddenly filled instantly with warmth and gratitude. The kind of warmth that makes you feel God's presence so strong in people, with whom barley know you, that he puts in your path at the right time!

Of all places this happened, it was at work.

Now it isn't like work is filled with robots. It is just that normally, working relationships don't touch that deep a level of kindness one would expect. Her act of kindness did not stop there as I was talking about my son's birthday another time and we were laughing about how he is excited to buy his own birthday gift this time around.

Out of the blue, she brings another envelope to me with a birthday card and $40 bill for Nicholas to buy himself a gift.

When it comes to giving, it is the act that is most appreciated. Sincere kindness is the most treasured and can be the most often missed in our lives.

Seriously, the magnitude of her actions leaves me speechless every single time. How do you thank someone like this? How to you express and let them know that they have touched your heart profoundly in every interaction with them? Not a gift or a card will ever explain what my heart feels for this young woman.

She would always stop by after this and check in with me, she would check and stay in touch not for any other purpose than to lend an ear to ease my pain.

For what I lack in words, I will try to make up in deeds.

I want her to know that this blog is to honor her, how special she is to me. I want her to know she has eased my pain and provided me with comfort when I needed the most.

I want her to know that because of her I believe that goodness still exists when you least expect it.

You are special to me because you are an angel that God has put in my path for a reason. Your kindness, friendship and warmth has touched me in so many ways and I cherish you and the memories we have shared.

A new challenge lies ahead. Leaving those who have given kindness a deeper meaning in my world.

As I move on to a new chapter, I must admit leaving to join another financial organization was very hard for me because these are the people I met as strangers, colleagues and have now become friends and family to me.

I am a proud Libra and that's how we do things. We feel deeply and strong for our friends! It hurts to know that I won't see them every day, but I want you to know you have made every moment and year spent so much more valuable and worth it for me.

I have grown as person so much more, because of you.

I know there many women out there that may have had my experience and many interactions as such. This particular experience is one that fills my heart every time. I decided to honor this woman the only way I knew how, in this blog.

To you my friend, God bless you and your family. Always know that you have a heart of gold. Rejoice in the goodness of your heart! May you stay healthy and happy, living a life of joy always and forever!

I received a gift of deep appreciation. I do promise to ease the pain of another.

Remember those moments, fill your cup, and add them to your bucket of "blessings & gratitude".

Chapter Five

TRANSPARENCY - DON'T MAKE IT PERSONAL AND YOU WILL THRIVE!

Quite some time ago, I had an assignment working for an executive that spoke a lot about transparency among teams and employees.

I decided to write this blog to summarize my own observations, learnings and takeaways on the topic of transparency.

When you're transparent, you reveal that you have nothing to hide...Basically, in the eyes of others, your 'brand' is that of an honest credible person.

Observations- Whenever the executive spoke, whether in meetings, events etc., employees where completely in tune. He was very articulate, always had the buy-in of the group and commanded any room allowing him the opportunity to speak. It was great to listen to and learn from him. Everyone in the room listened with admiration (dare I say adoration?) to this executive. He was always on the list to be invited to all sorts of engagement and events. Boy he had nailed the motivation and transparency talk down to a 'T'.

He was willing to confront subjects where no other executives within the organization were willing to tackle. He would take on topics such as honesty, glass ceiling, diversity, teamwork, cultures, and challenging the status quo. Everyone that knew him was inspired by him and wanted to take a page from the book of this executive.

As time passed, like most organizations, changes in leadership roles (a.k.a. re-orgs) will happen. For this executive, the change within the organization impacted his career goals as he was not moved forward on the previous two occasions.

With the changes delaying his progression, his message of "transparency" talks had begun to follow his mood and changed over time as well. Transparency in his books now changed from open and upfront, to delivering only certain information & doing so when it and if, it suited his agenda and goals.

Example #1: Promoted to all teams that everyone can grow in the company. Spoke of his plans to grow as well. Once his career path slowed significantly, his tone changed to advising the teams to 'suck it up', grow in your current roles and be proud of where you are.

Example #2: Spoke to all team members of being able to be promoted and that he is always available for open and honest dialogue. In reality, openings were filled from outside the depts. along with no notification to the current team so they may apply.

When you're transparent, you reveal that you have nothing to hide. This in-turn invites trust from your peers etc. Basically, in the eyes of others, your 'brand' is that of an honest credible person. It is not without its challenges though, as the prospect of being open and vulnerable may make you nervous at times. For some, the digital world has made observing transparency, an inescapable option.

***It's about always being honest,
irrespective of the outcome***

Learnings - What I've learned about *transparency*, is that it's about always being honest irrespective of the planned outcome. It is not when it suits the situation. If you are going to use it when it suits your agenda, overtime, people will take notice. As such the pulling and/or hiding of transparency card does not help one's personal brand in the long run. It may also affect your corporate brand if left unchecked. Specifically, if all along that's what you have been selling people on….it will uncover itself when confronted by reality.

Transparency is about understanding what's at stake and being able to speak the truth, no matter what the outcome is. Unless you are ready to be brave, step out courageously and be seen in the arena with your employees, team members, friends and people in general, you can't use it on a part-time basis or on your terms. It's either that you are fully transparent, or you are not! Don't advertise it if you can't always sell it consistently.

Your brand integrity will suffer, you will lose your followers & believers, you will become nothing other than someone who lives a life of double standards, in values, morals that only suit themselves rather than for the greater good.

To make room for vulnerability when no one wants to.

Takeaways - My takeaway from an observational standpoint and having the fortune of sitting on both sides of the leadership table are shared below.

What Transparency is to me:

- Honest, honesty and more honesty without limitations. The facts will help, not hinder the course for open dialogue.
- Tangible actions that have followed by inspired words, commitments, and promises
- Speaking the truth, free of judgment, criticisms, deceits or manipulations.
- Intent is pure
- Willingness to be in discomfort for sake of growth personally and professionally
- It's courage so there is no room for fear
- To believe or stand for something when no one else does
- Is change for the greater good
- To lead by example always
- To understand what's at stake, and choose to do the right thing
- To make room for what's acceptable & equal
- To educate, teach and inspire in all facets of life
- It's humility at its best!

- Consistent words followed by one's actions, values, and moral beliefs
- To make room for vulnerability when no one wants to.
- It's confidence for breaking free
- It's a long-life process to live by

What Transparency is not to me:

- Enlarged and inflated egos
- Put downs or tear downs of people
- Convenient for when/how/who/and what
- It's not part-time use
- It's not just using inspiring words, optimized to attract followers
- Does not allow room for lies, manipulations or deceits
- It is not a betrayal
- Something that makes you flip flop sides to save yourself
- Selfish
- It's not situational, either you are fully in or fully out
- A false brand – it is your 'Brand', so if using it, use it wisely and carefully
- It is not to be used cloaked as Diplomacy. It will always create an unstable foundation this way
- It's not made up stories to sell as realities and truth

If you are going to use transparency as your brand, be careful how it compares to the majority.

If you are going to use transparency as your brand, you must be careful as to how your interpretation of transparency, compares to what it means to the majority.

In the workplace, we tend to face some realities and situations that will alter our views, as we continue to climb the corporate ladder in our quest to attain the highest level of success professionally. For some though, they are unable to see the chaos and debris left behind in their quest for higher accomplishments and excellence.

Therefore, either you are fully transparent, or you are not. But you can't be both! So, chose one and stick with it, at least that way you don't have to worry about your brand image or continuing to conduct damage control for the long run.

Chapter Six

**MOVING BEYOND DISCOURAGEMENT –
UPLIFTING YOURSELF SPIRITUALLY
@WORK**

*He gives power to the weak, and to those
who have no might, He increases strength.
Isaiah 40:29 NKJV*

Why bring God and work together? Should they be two separate things? To be successful in life one is asked to observe certain consistencies across the board, so to speak. Work is work, home is home and faith belongs at home.

This is not a call to rise up but simply to point out that your strength inside, through your faith personally, is the same strength that will help you professionally at the office in times of emotional need.

Will your spiritualist belief carry you through tough times at work? You bet it does!

As a Christian, I have many reasons to celebrate God; Christ has risen, and we humbly know that we are the sheep of his flock. Yet sometimes, even the most devout believers may become discouraged, pretty much like how I feel some days.

After all, we live in a world where expectations can be high, and demands can be even higher.

Does our spiritual belief protect us from feelings of being let down by others or ourselves? It does not. This is where the 'keeping the faith' part kicks in.

When we fail to meet the expectations of others, or for that matter the expectations that we have for ourselves, we may be tempted to abandon hope.

To be honest, I am guilty of that many times myself. I was put in situations where I felt God had abandoned me, left sinking and barely keeping my head above water.

Until recent years, that is how I felt. I would speak to God and say "why have you left me? Why don't you hear me anymore? Are you testing me to the point where I come to lose my faith? Is that what you want me to do?"

My grace is sufficient for you, for my strength is made perfect in weakness.
2 Corinthians 12:9 NKJV

Over time my questions to God became pleas; "God, I love you and I don't want to be tested to my breaking point, because I am afraid that I won't follow you anymore! I fear the moment I do that I will lose my foundation, my values, and what I have been taught as child".

I was taught to always be faithful to my Father in heaven. Only He will see me through my darkest hours, to lean on God's understanding and not my own.

Why was I was taught that if you rely on humans they will always fail you, except God, who will make ALL things new. Will all humans fail me personally and professionally?

The reality is that yes, some people will fail you, BUT NOT ALL people will fail you. I have learned that God speaks through those who do believe in his faith.

It is through those whose advice and assistance has guided my actions towards improving my life as a woman and ultimately in my career as a professional.

I begged God in prayers not to let my fears and worry overwhelm me, because even though the bible says that fear produces courage and faith produces hope. I was failing miserably on all of it. All I wanted for me and my family was a break! But God had other plans. He knows exactly how he intends to use us. Our task is to remain faithful until he does.

> **The Lord is the one who will go before you. He will be with you; He will not leave you or forsake you. Do not be afraid or discouraged.**
> **Deuteronomy 31:8 HCS"**

> **At work or at home, seeking solace in your faith will give you strength to deal with your current challenges.**

If you 're a woman who has become discouraged with the direction of your day or your life (like I was), turn your thoughts and prayers to God.

He is a God of possibility, not negativity. He will help you count your blessings instead of your hardships.

Then, with a renewed spirit of optimism and hope, you can properly thank your Father in heaven for His blessings, for His love, and for His son.

When we reach the end of our strength, wisdom, and personal resources, we enter the beginning of His glorious provisions.

***I have reached all of that, and I am tired of fighting against the waves to survive, I am now defeated on my own.
I come to you Father to seek refuge
-Amal Candido***

Have you reached all of that just like me? Let's take refugee together in HIM.

Dear Lord, help me to do better by reminding me to come to you for strength. When my responsibilities seem overwhelming, and when I can't keep my head above water. To trust you to give me courage and perspective. I pray that you give me eyes like yours, to see your grace in every situation and to look to you as the ultimate source of my strength, my hope, my peace and my salvation. Amen.

Faith is not to be compartmentalized and left in a box when you head off to work each day. It is your faith that is the greatest source of strength and energy to overcome any and all obstacles in your way.

That faith within yourself, with God, combined with your commitment to your objectives, will always achieve the goals you set out for yourself.

I leave you with one of my favorite verses in the bible that I grew up on:

Come to me, all you who are weary and burdened, and I will give you rest. Take my yoke upon you and learn from me, for I am gentle and humble in heart, and you will find rest for your souls. For my yoke is easy and my burden is light.
Matthew 11:28

Chapter Seven

MIND, BODY AND SPIRIT WELLNESS - CONSIDER IT AN 'ANYTIME' SPRING CLEANING

A couple of years ago I was having difficulty on a personal level. I was at a stage in my life where I felt burnt out, unfulfilled, and my stress level and anxiety were through the roof! Wellness? I don't think so!

There was this special woman, a colleague, a confidante who treated me like her own daughter and grew to become my closest & wisest friend.

She cared so much about me and empathized with me through all my trials and tribulations.

One day in the midst of this messy time, she had asked, "Have you ever tried Yoga?" I smiled and said to her "You know I hate exercising. It's just not my thing and besides, I don't have the time to do it anyway."

Patiently she began to educate me on Yoga and convinced me that all I need is 20 mins a day, and I could do it on the weekends if I wanted.

She told me about how her husband is into meditation and I should investigate that as well, as it's all about living mindfully.

She added that it will help provide me with clarity and calmness if I really started to get into it.

I must admit she tried everything in her power to help me find my inner awareness, my triggers, and how to control my anxieties and thoughts.

She was without fail, so patient and determined that she bought me this book that I had fell in love with almost immediately called "You Can Heal Your Life", filled with amazing daily affirmations. I have it listed on the 'books I love' section on my website (www.myEAblog.com) ... (full-disclosure...I make NOTHING for any book mentioned. I want you to know what helped me, so that in case it may do the same for you). Back to my story now!

She looked up Yoga websites, YouTube vids and printed yoga poses to help me with the back pain I was having, no doubt from the stress. Oh, she did not stop there either. She would send me daily text messages, of encouraging quotes that she searched on Pinterest, for me to read each morning.

She was and is, my biggest supporter personally and professionally and an amazing friend, whom I adore and admire immensely.

Most days I ask myself "what would I have done without her?"

Mind you it was not as easy at the beginning to get close to her. She was a very private person and ensured her professionalism at work kept it that way.

But deep down, I knew I needed to get close to her because I saw (or maybe felt) qualities in her that I secretly wished I could someday be just like her. I was admiring her wisdom and smarts.

Eventually when we grew closer, she was happily coaching and teaching me the ropes of how to be a "kick ass" EA.

Believe me, she taught me a lot. One of the many tips I got to learn from my 'office sensei' was the "shift delete" method for peace of mind.

I just love how it takes away unnecessary noise in any given day...... that's about as far as I can say on that, it's an inside joke that I will keep as such sorry!

Anyhow, she also knows how much I give to others and never have time for myself. She suggested that I go on a mini getaway to relax and escape all the family crisis and noise that is around me. Her advice was for me to find time alone to be in my own company. I needed to balance my mind, body and spirit. She could see I was being too hard on myself and not kind to myself during this time.

At one point she told me, "Your love bucket is on empty. You can't think that you are able to give or receive love when yours is on empty."

Her words fell on me like a ton of bricks. "For Amal to be happy, and healthy," she started, "you must understand yourself. You must spend time with you and you need to find things that will reignite that energy inside of you."

"Amal, what do you like to do? How do you like to spend time?"

I knew right then I found out my best friend was also my counselor, psychologist and psychic all together as one! She was one of those rare friends, who was able to hear your story and carry the burden of the situation with you.

I had listened and set out on a mission. I found this place called "Grail Springs Wellness Retreat". Oh yes, this place was unique and different. A total departure from Amal-land! I had an amazing peaceful time there. It was like a two-day detox from anyone and anything in the the world around you. Best investment made in me ever!

This place was about empowerment, by taking charge of the one thing you have control over in life, your inner self. Your beliefs and attitudes color all that happens to you. Why not play the hand you were dealt with more awareness?

It begins with a decision to get to know yourself better and to take care of yourself on all levels: physical, emotional, mental, and spiritual. A well-nourished self is creative, energetic, joyful, giving; has rich, meaningful relationships and is continually growing.

I am blessed to have her in my life and am definitely a better person for it. I am convinced my journey would not have begun and the repercussions of which would have been devastating. Faith brought her to me at the right time in my life, where I would share, where I would listen and when I would begin the journey needed to improve my life and in turn, hopefully those close to me as well.

To that end, I would like to say Thank You my dearest, from the deepest part of me.

So, now towards the end of such a long journey, with my biggest supporter cheering me on to continue the discovery and finding balance in my life, I have stumbled on a few things that I thought might help others as well. It begins with a couple definitions of Self-Esteem that I have found listed below, during times of self-reflection.

"Self-Esteem, on a subtle and often unconscious level, is an emotion, how warm and loving you actually feel toward yourself, based on your individual sense of personal worth and importance. It is how you feel about yourself."
L.S. Barksdale, Building Self-Esteem

"Self-esteem is how you feel about yourself, based upon your personal evaluation of yourself. You consciously and unconsciously send thoughts, opinions, and images of yourself to yourself. Your perceptions, beliefs, and
self-concept may or may not be accurate.
Suzanne E. Harrill, Enlightening Cinderella Beyond the Prince Charming Fantasy

There were many useful resources that helped me, get out of my stuck mindset. Two of which I will be sharing below. It helps to be able to spend time with yourself and take a closer look.

Taking stock of your life, people, situations, your daily environment, the mental and physical condition of your heart every now and then, is important to the process of eliminating the toxins out of your life.
Consider it an annual spring cleaning that you can do as often as you choose.

See this checklist that I use to look so often on:

Signs of High Self-Esteem

- Having an internal locus of control, getting 'okayness' from within, not from others.

- Taking care of yourself – physically, emotionally, mentally, and spiritually.

- Maintaining a balance between extremes of thought, feeling, and behavior. When out- of-balance, taking action to correct.

- Learning from mistakes and being able to say, "I made a mistake." If it involves another person, being able to make amends or say, "I'm sorry." Able to forgive self and others.
- Managing your life responsibly.
- Honoring individual differences among people.
- Listening to other points of view.
- Taking responsibility for your own perceptions and reactions; not projecting onto others.
- Having the ability to listen to your wise inner self (your intuition), and to act on this guidance.
- Knowing your own strengths and weaknesses.
- Choosing continuous self-improvement and taking positive risks.
- Balancing being and doing.
- Feeling warm and loving towards self.
- Giving and receiving love easily, with no strings attached.
- Demonstrating self-respect, self-confidence, and self-acceptance.

Signs of Low Self-Esteem

• Self-blame, self-criticism, or constantly putting others down through guilt, blame, shame, or faultfinding. Finding forgiveness difficult.

• Over- or under-achieving, -eating, -working, -doing, etc.

• Playing the victim, rationalizing that outside circumstances are the causes of your problems.

• Not taking responsibility for your own life; turning power over to another to make decisions for you, then feeling victimized if the results are not to your liking.

- Taking too much responsibility for the lives of others, dominating and making decisions for them.
- Fear of change and reluctance to take risks. Or too much change, taking dangerous, unwise risks.
- Constant negativity or being so optimistic that reality is denied.
- Reacting to others with extreme emotion or no emotion.
- Boastfulness, lying, embellishing, exaggerating, and overbearing behavior around others.
- Inability to maintain integrity during interactions with others.
- Demanding to be "right," needing to have agreement or have your own way most of the time, or constantly acquiescing to the will and opinions of others.
- Constantly comparing yourself to others, thereby feeling inferior or superior.
- Black/white, either/or thinking; e.g., believing that a person is either good or bad based on rigid standards of behavior.
- Having pervasive deep-seated feelings of fear, terror, or panic.
- Speaking with lots of shoulds, oughts, could haves, and yes, buts.
- Interpreting the hurtful words or actions of others as proof of your unworthiness.

Ways to Improve Your Self-Esteem

1. *Change your negative self-talk* - Everyone has a voice inside her/his mind that is continually commenting. The negative, critical, hurtful comments need to be changed. Begin listening to what you say to yourself and then talk back to your negative self-talk with the truth. Speed up the process by saying positive statements or affirmations; such as, "I like myself and am a worthwhile person, I forgive myself for not knowing/being/doing..., I deserve love, inner peace, and fulfillment." Make a cassette tape, in your voice, of affirmations. Listen daily.

2. *Visualize* what you want to create in your life - Picture what you want to create, whether it is a new dress or feeling confident in new situations. When you combine an affirmation, with deep feeling, and with a positive mental picture you add power to what you want to create. Look for pictures in magazines that picture what you want to create and glue them into your journal.

3. *Nurture yourself* - Take care of yourself physically, emotionally, mentally, and spiritually. Enjoy the times when others can nurture you or meet your needs; watch the tendency to set yourself up for disappointment with unreal expectations.

4. *Build a support system* - You deserve to have at least one person to talk to who accepts you without judging you. Consider joining a group to meet new people.

5. *Take time to be alone daily* - Spending quality time alone allows you to listen to your inner self. It is time to think, read, write, pray, meditate, or listen to your intuition.

6. *Use your talents* - Develop your interests. Take classes, find a teacher to begin.

7. *Keep a journal* - Writing is a good way to get to know yourself, solve your problems, lower your stress level, and balance yourself emotionally. If you have never written before, begin by writing for 20 minutes a day for the duration of this course. Include your thoughts, feelings, and emotional reactions to people and situations that have upset or hurt you. Eventually, insights and wisdom, that under normal circumstances are hidden from you, flow onto the paper. Do not worry about spelling or grammar. Consider using different colored inks. Writing clarifies your thoughts, feelings, needs, wants, visions, values, goals, and priorities and helps you communicate better with others. Following are questions to get you started.

Credit: Suzanne E. Harrill, M.Ed., Counselor, Teacher, Author: Innerworks

I would like to leave you with my favorite part of Suzanne E. Harrills' work. This was an eye opener and helped me tremendously through my journey - see next: **Self Care Chart and Medicine Wheel.**

Mind Body and Spirit Wellness
60 ways for self-care

Look over this list, I want you to put a check mark beside all the things that you currently do (in the last month).

Then I want you to look at the list, look at the selves (mental, emotional, physical, spiritual) and find the one category that has the least amount of check marks in it. This is the self you should start working on first. For example, if body had 3 checkmarks, and the rest had 3 or more, this would be the self you want to focus on first.

After you have found the self that has the least amount of checkmarks, I want you to circle three things in that column that you're willing to try.

Now find the next self that has the least and so on and so forth. When you are done, you will have your selves rated from 1-4, one being the most important, four being the last. You will have three things you're willing to try for every self.

At this point, write the three things you're willing to try for each self, into the appropriate circle in the medicine wheel below.

When you are done the medicine wheel, it will be your new goal sheet for your self-care!! You can post this some place you will see it often, such as your fridge for example.

Credit: Suzanne E. Harrill, M.Ed., Counselor, Teacher, Author: Innerworks

PHYSICAL	EMOTIONAL	MENTAL	SPIRITUAL
Take a walk	Deep breath and think" I am calm and peaceful	Say an affirmation	Connect with Nature.
Ride a bike	Share feelings about an experience with a friend	Read a book or magazine article	Concentrate on the flame of a candle.
Soak in a hot bath with candles and music	Listen to music you like	Express your thoughts & feelings in a journal	meditate
Exercise at the gym	Sing or makes sounds	Make a to do list	Pray.
Stretch and move to music	Hug someone or ask for a hug	Write a poem	Talk to your guardian angel.
Practice Yoga postures	Pet your dog or cat	Write a letter	Listen to a guided meditation tape.
Take a course in Tai Chi, water aerobics or yoga	Talk to someone by pretending they are facing you in an empty chair	Listen to tapes	Write about your spiritual purpose.

Sit in the sun for 15 minutes	Telephone a long distance friend or relative	Email a friend	Visualize yourself in a peaceful place.
Change one thing to improve your diet	Notice what you are feeling several times a day	List things you will do to improve your life	Do something of service for another or for your community.
Watch birds and animals interact in nature	Write a letter to someone who has hurt you but do not send it	Update negative beliefs that limit your life	Join a church group.
Go swimming	Feel your fear and take a positive risk for change	Journal write daily about your reactions thoughts and feelings for a month	Learn about a religion different from your own.
Sit in a garden or park	Smile at a stranger and send them thoughts of peace acceptance joy	List your traits needs and want	Study with a spiritual teacher.
Take a nap	Affirm yourself daily	Make a list of short term and long term goals	Study ancient esoteric wisdom teachings.
Get a massage	Watch children play talk to your inner child in a loving joyful way	Preview your day upon awakening Review upon retiring	Practice unconditional love and forgiveness with self and others.
Eat totally healthy for one day	Acknowledge yourself for accomplishments you are proud of	Work on your family tree	Practice a daily quiet time routine to connect spiritually.

Family Wellness and Youth in Distress
Lesson 4: Self Esteem

Handout 4-B
Asset Mapping Page 3 of 3

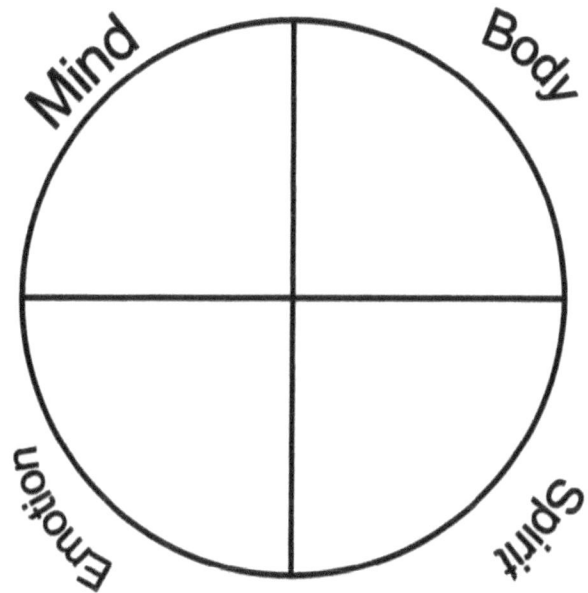

**Credit: Suzanne E. Harrill, M.Ed., Counselor,
Teacher, Author: Innerworks**

Chapter Eight

THE ROOKIE EA - THOUGHTS AND TIPS TO MAKE IT THROUGH THE DAY

I met with an executive who was hiring at the time, he could tell I was a rookie...

Years ago, when I started as an Executive Assistant, I was placed in a job by a staffing company. I was totally new to this role; I must admit I had no idea what to expect. For my first temporary job placement, I met with an executive who was hiring at the time, he could tell I was a rookie with no prior experience in the role before. The Executive was hesitant to hire me for two reasons, one being that I was stay at home mom for the past few years and secondly I appeared too young. That alone was his indication that I knew nothing about the role and won't be able to rise to the challenge.

It is rare to ever hear 'the reasons why I didn't get hired' but I was lucky enough to learn why later on.

Fast forward, he ended up hiring a recommended 'seasoned' EA that as it turned out, was not a good fit and did not do a good job. As office politics go, it was one of the classic recommendations made from co-worker EA's that wanted someone they knew to be hired rather than someone most qualified.

Food for Thought: Sometimes it is as simple as a choice made that you had zero chance of influencing. The goal is to keep focused on the big picture and persevere. You will find something. Maybe not necessarily on your time but keep the faith because with your efforts, it will happen!

> **A few weeks later I was called back by the recruiter, asking me if I would consider working for this executive even though he rejected me earlier.**

A few weeks later I was called back by the recruiter, asking me if I would consider working for this executive even though he rejected me earlier. I needed the money so who am I to be picky and choosy. I accepted my challenge and hoped for the best.

This experience was an amazing entry to the world of an EA. For me it felt like a concerted and chaotic crash course into what an Executive Assistant job entails. Without any guidance, or prior experience or a network to lean on for resources and help (yup, it sounds crazy as I didn't even research online to find out what's out there that could provide some sort of guidelines, tips or tricks to support me). I was not thinking at the time, I was in the "doing mode" and proving myself mode.

You may ask the question "about other EAs that were working in the company, how come they did not help me?" Well I have lots of answers for that; this company had a very strange EA culture. It was not about helping another, or sharing best practices, or helping a new fellow EA to ramp up quickly. It was more about proving they are better than YOU!

Food for Thought: Now I did not go in completely blind. I did have great experience in hospitality to deal with stress and the variety of personality types. Part of that background also included basic administrative duties in certain roles.

At the beginning I thought to myself "Wow these individuals are really interested to learn about me."

Let the show begin! Most of the EA's I interacted with were too curious about where I was before. What had I done prior to joining the role? How long my contract is for? (too concerned with sizing me up).

At the beginning I thought to myself "Wow these individuals are really interested to learn about me."

I did not realize it was a info gathering session for them to help support the process of bringing me down, since they have thought to themselves "am not good enough, and I don't know what am doing anyway so it should be easy to blame the mistakes, and pile up the workload that no one wants to do on the new EA."

Food for Thought: Everyone wants to impress. There will be times that you will step into roles where the 'lifers' (long tenured staff) will want to 'mold' you. They will want to know everything about you and then slowly let you know how things are 'done' here. Your goal is to focus on your efforts to keep your boss working smoothly. Clear the noise coming from the gabby Greta's and keep moving forward. If you want to discuss this further, let me know as this is a blog unto itself!

I had earned the right to become a full-time employee from starting out as a contractor.

The truth is I am grateful for this experience as it helped me see the good, the bad, and the ugly in a very short time. I have learned so much and managed to overcome many challenges thrown my way.

I had earned the right to become a full-time employee from starting out as a contractor. I have survived multiple company restructures and supported my fair share of different executives over the years.

I am standing (ok, sitting as I type this), today very proud of myself, despite some of my former colleagues who still see me as a rookie, lacking the seasonality. I have been challenged by individuals with the classic traditional mind-set of secretaries versus how the Executive Assistant role has evolved over the years.

I was young, eager and wanting to prove myself. My efficiency, speed, directness, along with my friendly demeanor and willingness to be helpful would be considered both my strength and weakness.

All the extra work and owning up to my mistakes along the way add to those attributes equally. The more I accomplished the more I ended up with more challenges, insecurities, bad politics and faced those mind games from the gabby Greta's tearing my performance down.

If you are starting out, you need to hear about the fun and not so fun stuff. That's why I feel this blog is worth writing about - BUT I have no intention of sharing all the ugly that I had to experience. However, what I would like to share are some of the learning tips that I have come away with.

If you are a new EA, trying to find your way and earn the respect of colleagues alike, understand that you will meet people who will help you out, as well as people who will want to see your performance suffer to their benefit. How you navigate through all the 'firsts' at the beginning of your career will determinate your survival rate, learning and building of your brand.

Being an EA is such a rewarding career, however most of you will need to go through a few valleys first before you reap the rewards.

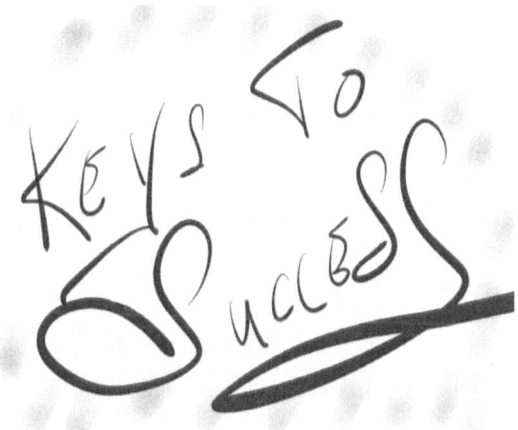

In conclusion I am happy to share my personal thoughts & tips that helped me through it all, when you are new and trying to build your credibility below are the things that helped and worked for me:

- Understand and define what is your role to the success of the Executive and department you are supporting

- Get to know other Executive Assistants within your department/area. Find out about their experience, who they have supported in the past, how long they have worked in the company and what other tasks & duties that are divided/shared among them.

- Determinate if your role is over-lapping with other peers
- Understand what the expectations are of you by the role or from your Executive. Or determinate the process of defining expectation if none are in place.
- Know your Executive, and what works well for them
- Don't be shy to say "No" (it was one of my personal down-falls early on, especially when you are new)
- Build a network of EAs for support, if not possible internally then look externally for support
- Google - is your best friend for almost everything!
- Microsoft Office and Googles G-Suite are your tickets to stardom
- Communication is your key to success; understand the different types of communication within your organization and which ones works well. (let me know if you want a separate blog on this one...it's huge!)
- When it comes to learning people's names; your org chart, phone directory, and global distribution lists and intranet are your guide

- Knowledge is your power – so pace yourself and get acquainted with company's website, look up policies and training manuals etc. If not just for yourself, they will come in handy in case your boss needs help.

- Identify and introduce yourself to key individuals & partners such as; finance, HR, office manager, building tenanted services, IT, receptionist, communication, help desk, direct reports along with some of the movers & shakers within the organization etc.

- Duties as assigned – this one is a biggie you will find it listed in every EA job description. It is a broad statement with the possibility that "EVERYTHING" will fall under it. So, try to get as much clarity as possible or at least a benchmark. (and hope for the best!)

- Floor plan – to help with tours & detours on your first few weeks on the job (those floor maps/plans will help you to know who sits where? So, you can find people easier at the beginning)

- Vacation coverage/sick days/and off-sites – what are the protocols in place? If none, create them.

- Joining meetings, managing inbox and scheduling 1 on 1's are very important in establishing and creating great work habits, opportunities for learning and relationship building with your Executive.

- Observation, active listening skills and even more observation – are the powerful ones that have helped me succeed time and time again and are my key strengths which I was able to develop well over time.

- There are plenty of strategies that work best and are not inconclusive of the list above which is my personal favorite. Best of luck to all the new Executive Assistants out there, be brave, stay calm, remain confident in your ability, stay humble, decide what is your brand and build it with grace.

Chapter Nine

THREE CORE LEADERSHIP QUALITIES NEEDED TO MAKE A POSITIVE CHANGE

Good leaders help guide us, make the tough calls that keep organizations, companies and countries moving forward. Determining whether moving forward is beneficial or harmful depends on the leader's ability to recognize if their actions will impact other in beneficial or harmful way.

We can spot a bad leader almost immediately. Our society has proven quite adept at this.

The question here is, can we spot a good leader and what is it exactly that would make a good leader?

Positive Leadership requires action (**focus**), provides direction (**vision**), and inspires (**character**).

Pay careful attention to your bodies internal signals

The first Core Leadership Quality is **Focus**. Self-Awareness, to look within oneself and listen to your inner voice. Those who heed their inner voice ultimately make better decisions as they will use this connection with your 'real self' to elicit resources or clarity in decision making. It is a concept not easily explained so let's dive into an example here.

Pay careful attention to your bodies internal signals. These are physiological changes, very subtle, that your brain does notice with concentration. This area of your brain, tucked behind your frontal lobes is known as the insula. Sit still and tune into the insula by focusing on your heartbeat. With practice, you will recognize this and other "stories" your body tells you.

Communication is the ultimate key to this qualities' success

The second Core Leadership Quality is **Vision**. Make a draft of your goal(s). Share with with others. Refine it using feedback and support your vision with commitment and inspiration that moves you personally.

Now try it out with colleagues. Ask your colleagues/team to create a vision and share with each other. This will definitely build trust as you discover how to capitalize on what drives each individual and use strength in diversity as a major competence.

Communication is the ultimate key to this qualities' success.

Positive delivery, placing a high value on two-way communication, meet often if needed, over communicate and choosing the right words by knowing your audience will support your Vision.

The social conscience of your leadership character is brought forward by being mindful of your integrity, honesty, loyalty and selflessness as a leader.

The third Core Leadership Quality is **Character**. Respectfulness of others and your beliefs, fairness, cooperation, compassion and humility are the traits you use to bring out this skill.

The self-discipline and courage of taking action on your vision, the passion used to achieve acceptance of your goals, brought forth by the wisdom and competence gained from experience will be used to transform the strength of your leadership.

The social conscience of your leadership character is brought forward by being mindful of your integrity, honesty, loyalty and selflessness as a leader.

Leaders more accustomed to giving input rather than being attentive will have trouble with any of the above. Be wary of the 'noise' distracting the path to achieving your vision. Leaders who stay true to their personal values are known to succeed better in the long run.

You must believe in and practice these three Leadership Qualities and be aware that the outcome will benefit yourself, those around you and others you may not meet, without negative impact or consequences.

Chapter Ten

@HOME AND @WORK SERIES – HELPING THE MIND AND BODY.

I wrote the following short passages in an effort for you to open a conversation with yourself. The following information is not intended as medical/therapeutic advice as much as it is a collection of thoughts and experience assembled in various categories I've identified that has helped me over the years.

I've included space for notes you can make to use with respect to your own journey if it helps.

Better @Home and @Work – 5 ways of dealing with anxiety

Most people do not like to admit when they are feeling anxious. However, in reality, everyone in the world experiences several nail-biting moments that can make them apprehensive.

Some levels of stress and anxiety can actually be good for you because they can encourage you to take a path towards change and growth. But when the stress and anxiety are extended they can become an overbearing burden and can even impact your health negatively.

Fear and anxiety can last for a short time, but the feelings are supposed to pass eventually. When they do not, these emotions can take over your life and affect your capacity to operate at work, sleep, eat, travel and enjoy life in general.

It is important to deal with anxiety to prevent a repetitive cycle from occurring. Here are some simple tips to help you deal with your anxiety:

Remember that you are not alone
Whenever you are going through anxiety, it helps to keep in mind that you are not alone. Anxiety is a part of normal life, and everyone goes through it especially after moments of stress. It helps when you admit to yourself that you are anxious because it happens even to the best of us.

You can handle things easily by getting a loved one involved or someone that has gone through anxiety and dealt with it successfully. This person can act as your confidant and a source of empathy for what you are going through.

Face your fears if you can
If you tend to avoid difficult situations that make you anxious, it might cause you to stop doing the things that you want or need to.

If you can, try and test out a situation that causes you anxiety where possible because it will let you know what to expect. Anxiety issues tend to worsen when you choose to ignore them.

Know yourself
Try and learn more about yourself and where your issues with anxiety stem from to deal with them in the right way.

Consider keeping a diary or a thought record that notes down what happens when you are anxious. This is a useful technique for helping you to deal with and address the underlying issues that make you anxious.

Get plenty of sleep
Not getting sufficient sleep can make it harder to perform and it can also make it difficult to get through the rest of the day.

Try as much as you can to get least 8 hours of sleep each day as it will enable you to deal with your emotions much better.

Exercise

Exercise and physical activity can help to de-stress you and can give you an outlet to let out your emotions.

You can also use a broad array of tactics such as trying out a hobby or meditation.

These techniques are inexpensive, and they can help you get over your anxiety whenever you need to.

NOTES

**Better @Home and @Work –
5 ways to get you started on boosting your self-confidence**

Self-esteem issues and a terrible self-image can affect you in a range of different ways from changing how you view yourself and your relationships to how you treat others.

When dealing with self-esteem, some of the most common issues that you can expect and should overcome include:

Self-hate
While there are instances where you might dislike who you are, loathing every thought and action that you take is typically a sign of low self-esteem.

Self-hate is usually embodied by anger and frustration about your status in life and an inability to forgive yourself even for the smallest mistakes.

You can transform by changing your inner dialogue; the first step to silencing self-hate is by modifying the way that you talk to yourself. You can quiet those negative thoughts in your head by repeating affirming sentences and phrases that can encourage a positive response.

An obsession with being perfect

Perfectionism is one of those destructive tendencies that promote the spirit of low self-esteem and self-doubt to grow.

A perfectionist is an individual who lives in a perpetual state of failure because their accomplishments will never be impressive regardless of how good they are.

Whenever you go through this, you must always try and remember that there is a huge difference between being a failure and failing at something.

Try and set realistic goals by consciously assessing how manageable or reasonable your expectations are.

Here are 5 ways to get you started with your self-confidence

Live in the Moment
When you focus on living in the moment, you can select your moves and actions wisely. It is easier to make decisions because you will be unaffected by the mistakes of your past and you will most likely be unconcerned about the things that you cannot control in the future.

Another term for this is mindfulness.

Develop Awareness
When you develop a sense of awareness, you can recognize and respond to the events in your life as they happen. Awareness allows you to create a link between your actions and emotions which allows you to react healthily.

Try Meditation
Meditation enables you to let go and free yourself of all the harmful thoughts that may be racing in your mind. You need to recognize that your feelings are transient rather than part of who you are and meditation can help with this.

Learn to let go
Letting go of any petty things will allow you to develop mindfulness for yourself and others. When you let go of everything that you think you should be, you can trust your decisions to select what is right for you.

Show yourself compassion
You should show yourself love just as much as you show others. Self-compassion enables you to accept where you are in life and it lets you plan for where you need to be.

NOTES

**Better @Home and @Work –
The importance of professional growth through personal reading**

Contrary to popular belief, reading will never go out of fashion, despite the endless claims that it is quickly going out of style. True, reading is something that fewer people want to do.

However, it is a shame that people have lost their connection to literature because it has endless benefits for your health and wellbeing.

Throughout history, reading has always been an important component of social life; stories have been used to teach, entertain and share a message with others.

Ultimately, reading something can have a significant impact on the way that you choose to interact with the world. Here are some important reasons for reading for personal growth:

It enhances your empathy
Most stories, at least the good ones, have compelling protagonists, which are the main characters included in every story.

The reader, therefore, has to care about the protagonist in a relatable way, which helps to build empathy.

If you can learn to emote over someone fictional, then you will be a lot more equipped to handle individuals in real life.

It allows you to de-stress
Reading on a regular basis can help to reduce your stress levels by as much as 70 percent. Although activities such as listening to music and exercise have been known to help with anxiety, reading is one of the strongest techniques that a person can use.

It helps the mind and body relax, and it also contributes to distracting you constructively.

It is peaceful
Reading is a soothing activity like no other. Even for high-energy individuals, reading forces them to sit and be still, which can be miraculous for a person suffering from anxiety.

Also, reading can also be a form of therapy because it can give you answers that guide you on your personal problems.

The stories included in books can help to bring up your own unresolved conflicts, allowing you to tackle your issues in a much healthier way.

It increases your intelligence
This should come as no surprise, but reading on a consistent basis helps to boost your knowledge levels. Everything that you read, even the fiction pieces, fills your head with new information that can come in handy in tricky situations.

The more knowledge that one acquires, the better one can face a challenge head-on.

For memory improvement
When you read books, you have to recall an array of characters, their backgrounds, history, and the nuances that are included throughout every story. Reading regularly enables you to remember these components of stories with relative ease.

Every new memory created in your brain develops new brain pathways that strengthen the existing ones. The whole process eventually leads to long-term memory recall capability.

NOTES

Better @Home and @Work – How to deal with that inner struggle of self-doubt

Self-doubt is something that a lot of people have to deal with on a daily basis. At one point or another in an individual's life, it is quite normal to start doubting or asking questions about the state of things. Are you making enough money? Are you successful enough? Are you doing enough to be fruitful and healthy?

Because of these questions, it is easy to find yourself in a constant state of that inner struggle of self-doubt.

Everyone grapples with self-doubt, even some of the most successful people that you know. A little self-doubt is not only normal but healthy as well. It prevents you from crossing that fine line between being cocky and being self-confidence. However, although every one of us struggles with a little self-doubt, you must never allow that self-doubt to derail you from what you actually want to accomplish.

Self-doubt can be that persuasive and upsetting voice that persistently holds you back. So, what is the best way to overcome those incidences of self-doubt so that you can move forward?

Question your doubt

Faulty ways of thinking about yourself can be extremely harmful. So, you should test or challenge your doubts whenever they occur by asking yourself whether they are realistic or whether or not you might be overreacting.

Whenever you experience incidences of fear and self-doubt, it helps to spend time reflecting on the causes of the doubt.

Argue against some of the causes and challenge your beliefs to get the right answers. Your negative reactions might start to change causing you to reframe your mind and the situation.

Stop it immediately
Initially, when your inner struggles with self-doubt start, you should be quick to stop them immediately. This is because allowing them to persist can cause them to spin out of hand or grow into a steady stream of discouraging sentences.

Whenever the feelings start to bubble up, try and talk to that doubtful bit of yourself to discourage yourself from going down that road again.

By stopping feelings of self-doubt as they crop up, you can disrupt the destructive thought pattern from taking over. Recognize that self-doubt is not unique to you is also important because it means that you are not alone.

Keep your circle close
Whenever you are going through moments of self-doubt, you should keep your circle of friends or family members close to you. The people that you spend time with habitually can have a profound impact on you whether you are aware of it or not. Your friends and family can help to talk you down and make you feel calm, which can improve your perspective drastically.

NOTES

Chapter Eleven

FEAR AND EMOTIONAL PAIN THAT COMES WITH CHANGE

Do they happen together or come to us in stages when events occur? Is all change, bad change?

I have decided to write this one on fear and emotional pain that comes with change, focusing on the mixed emotions that they bring and how to cope with them as I have shared some real-life experiences in previous posts.

I spent most of my life trying to protect myself from emotional pain, hiding my fears and pretending that I can manage them with each change or life event.

For someone who went through such trouble to show people how resilient I can be, I must say I have learned nothing from my past hardships until very recently in my life.

To keep it short, I will give a brief breakdown on fear and emotional pain from change and their effects on the lessons learned in my life. Living in a country with deep political issues already, followed by the pain of my father's death at eight years old and living in survival mode, one would assume I would be a pro at handling change, pain and fear.

Each time there was a change, each time there was fear or pain, was followed up with a survival mode 'suck it up' mindset implanted in my brain. The result of this, was that my ability to navigate the emotions of fear and emotional pain from each change properly, would fail, for many years to come.

I have struggled repeatedly every time my life was affected by change, or pain, which invited fear into my heart. When you really think about it, we don't always organize our thoughts about emotions that well while 'in the moment'. Unless you are completely mindful 24/7 and have self-reflected through on the events that were past or are currently happening, dealing with your feelings while under the stress of change is generally difficult for any of us to manage alone.

As the saying goes "everything happens in life for a reason" I truly believe in that statement, however it's always easier said than done, than to understand and process methodically 'in the moment'!

Can you do change without pain or fear? Can you do fear without change? Can you feel pain without change, or fear? I don't believe so.... I believe they all play a part, either all the time or at once in our personal & professional life.

111

Change is inevitable, it's all around us. It's moving to a new country, joining a new company, moving to a new house, children growing up and leaving their parents nest, new relationship/or marriage etc. What I know for sure, is there are two sides to change, positive & negative. It's how you choose to cope with it that affects your outcome and views on the change you are experiencing.

I must admit my current change, leaving an organization that I was familiar with its culture and people, to joining a new organization, has not been an easy one, or a walk in the park so to speak. It probably explains why people who have worked longer than five years in a company don't jump ship that easily.

It's not just about the pension as most people I talked to explained, it's about shifting from everyday comfortable shoes to a new pair that will take so much effort to break in.

We are creatures of comfort and when, after a few years working, given the option of leaving the company, will not do so as you are already deeply ingrained with the culture and co-workers. Most employees will leave because of a bad boss but most employees will stay because of social circles within the company.

Change forces you to stretch yourself, it challenges your knowledge, skills and tests your patience. Another thing change does – it humbles you down to the core. It's not about what you know or what you have accomplished already. It's about how quick you can learn with an open mindset, versus a closed one. Change has one more quality in common with pain. It tests your stamina and brings vulnerability to the surface.

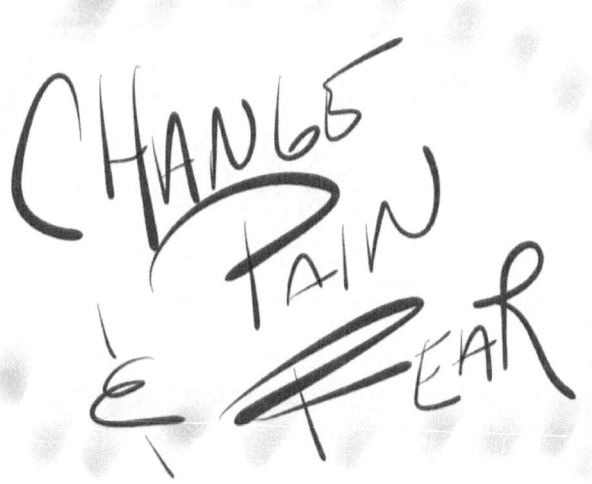

Fear is another emotion we can experience when we are going through change, or emotional pain. Being hurt in a relationship, fear of losing someone, fear of failing at a new job, fear of change from being out of our comfort zone and fear that brings shame, to name a few.

When you fear the pain and the change, you end up missing all the opportunities that present themselves to you. Fear delays you from taking risks, challenging your ability to grow. It has the opposite effect of moving forward. Fear paralyzes us.

Our society taught us that fear is shameful and a sign of weakness, but what we do know is that if channeled right, it produces perseverance and character.

The lesson I keep learning is that I can't outrun fear in order to accomplish anything. I must face my fears head on and hope for the best (relocation to a new country, buy a place, change jobs, have children, cancer scare, loss of loved ones, etc.).

We are here on this earth for a purpose and to get to our destination, we must go through all the complexity of emotions which is part of the refining process, of who we are meant to be.

Pain tends to bring all sorts of emotions to the forefront, with anger seemingly to be the most common one. Some pains are good for you! I know it sounds crazy, but you can't make it through life without pain and to reach contentment, peace and joy, you must go through the pain to get to the other side.

Some pain brings out the worst in people of course. But if you take a moment and look closely all around you, everyone has a story to tell that involves pain, losses, regrets, failures or addictions such as food, alcohol, drugs or sex.

When I reviewed my list I find that change, fear and pain all have shame and anger in common which places us in a vulnerable state. In a society that does not like to talk about shame or feelings of vulnerability, we are ultimately taught to suck it up, to get a thick skin.

The end result in most cases is the cycle repeating itself, leading us to teach our own children the same.

Don't talk about emotions, there is no place for emotions in the real world out there.

You need to show you are strong and hide weakness, you need to be a fighter, you need to be resilient.

Resilient? I need to be resilient? Did anyone stop and ask themselves how one becomes resilient? Technically resilience is the capacity to recover quickly from difficulties; toughness.

The more difficulties you have, the quicker your ability to spring back. The key words here are 'spring back'. Just how does one spring back? You can choose to bury the event or the fear and with a stiff upper lip, get back on your feet and move on.

This way is much faster as many have shown but, in the end, it will prevent you from experiencing deeper emotional connections etc to the extent you could have were you to have chosen the tougher road back.

That 'tougher road' back is going through the pain, through the change, through the fear. Being vulnerable, showing up and being seen.

The shear act of leaning into pain, the willingness to face that uncomfortable situation head on is what ultimately gives you the strength to spring back stronger and better able to deal with this situation, should it occur once more.

Nobody who breathes will tell you it was easy. It will always be harder to build resilience properly. Once you have dealt with the pain, not buried it, dealt with the fear, not to be kept hidden, you will transform to become a person of great strength inside.

I would like to share two amazing quotes by Dr. Brené Brown. Her message and her books have helped me a lot, her research on shame, for example, has made a tremendous impact with me:

"A lot of cheap seats in the arena are filled with people who never venture onto the floor. They just hurl mean-spirited criticisms and put-downs from a safe distance. The problem is, when we stop caring what people think and stop feeling hurt by cruelty, we lose our ability to connect. But when we're defined by what people think, we lose the courage to be vulnerable. Therefore, we need to be selective about the feedback we let into our lives. For me, if you're not in the arena getting your ass kicked, I'm not interested in your feedback."
— Brené Brown, Rising Strong

"Of all the things trauma takes away from us, the worst is our willingness, or even our ability, to be vulnerable. There's a reclaiming that has to happen."
— *Brené Brown, Rising Strong*

Lastly, if you can try to put into practice the Ten Guideposts for Wholehearted Living listed below: by — Brené Brown, Rising Strong

1. Cultivating authenticity: letting go of what people think
2. Cultivating self-compassion: letting go of perfectionism
3. Cultivating a resilient spirit: letting go of numbing and powerlessness
4. Cultivating gratitude and joy: letting go of scarcity and fear of the dark
5. Cultivating intuition and trusting faith: letting go of the need for certainty
6. Cultivating creativity: letting go of comparison
7. Cultivating play and rest: letting go of exhaustion as a status symbol and productivity as self-worth

8. Cultivating calm and stillness: letting go of anxiety as a lifestyle
9. Cultivating meaningful work: letting go of self-doubt and "supposed to"
10. Cultivating laughter, song, and dance: letting go of being cool and "always in control"
11. Hopefully you will find it as a helpful coping mechanism, into whatever you are facing in the present, past or future.

Chapter Twelve

WHAT HAVE YOU DONE TO HELP OTHERS IN NEED?

It was one of those days I had at work, where I felt nothing I do is good enough. It didn't matter how hard I worked or how I helped, the more tasks I took on to receive some sort of acknowledgment from my boss for the extra work, the more it fell on deaf ears and blind eye.

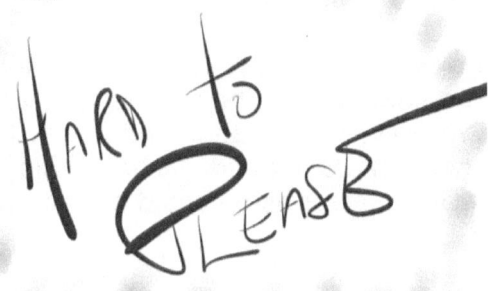

The reality was for me is that it did not matter what I did, I supported someone who was a self-centered individual. They lacked the sense of 'let's stop and think about rewarding or appreciating the employees that take on more responsibilities'.

Every time I have taken a task, event or project over and above, it was carried out in an effortless and flawless manner.

The result was, as I had been told long ago about taking on extra work, is it would go unappreciated and taken for granted.
Whatever the results and keeping positive, I was hoping for the opposite reaction I had received.

The story I am sharing with you today was on one of those days that I was feeling down. I came home hoping for an emotional uplift from my family.

I saw my son very quiet, so I asked him about school today. "Why the long face?" Nicholas started crying and told me that the kids in school don't like him.

He went on to say that he had a rough day at school in religion class. The teacher was asking the kids to share stories about what they have done to help others in need. Nicholas told me that he froze in class as he could not answer the question.

He felt incapable and started to cry in front of the whole class, because he realized he never helped anyone. In his own words this boy described himself as 'not good enough and lacks compassion'.

Nicholas explained, how could he be so selfish that he did not once stop to think about helping others who are in need. The tears kept rolling down his cheeks all the while as he tries to lick them so he can taste his salty tears. Kids and the things they do!

I realized right then, my son is in desperate need of comfort and understanding as he thinks he is this horrible human being.

It's ironic what God is trying to teach me in that moment through my son's hard day at school, which happened to be the same feeling I felt but, in this instance, my son needed the comfort more than me.

The lesson learned was that I needed to remind Nicholas that he is a loving child who was created with a higher purpose in life and God has a plan for his future.

I told Nicholas that while he may not understand, all he needed to be for now, is a child of God with an open heart and strong faith. Faith to believe in things he cannot see but walk in obedience with his Heavenly Father.

I went on to remind him that he does help those in need throughout the year. I reminded him about the times we donate toys, books, shoes and clothes to charity and church with and at times without him present.

The thing is every winter & summer at minimum, Nicholas and I go through all this toys, books, shoes and clothes that he has out grown, and we pile them up in bags for donations. This exercise happens throughout the year. He was taught from a young age that the simple act of donating, will bring happiness and joy to other kids who are in need.

He totally forgot about it mainly because he was only part of going through his items and putting them into bags. I realized it was my fault that I should have included him each time we take those items over to the church or a charity, so he can see what happens to them next.

I realized that I needed to point out to him that the acts of kindness and generosity that he does often, must have seemed like second nature and he did not even think to mention it.

This wonderful young boy seemed to misunderstand what an act of kindness looked like daily. In his mind, they had to be these big grand gestures of kindness to count.

So, as you can imagine as a mother I felt I failed him. How could he put such pressure on himself? Did I do that to him or was it society and social media that contribute to the feeling of inadequacy?

So, I decided to talk to him about some acts of kindness he has done and continues to do. It was apparent Nicholas needed a reminder of his actions of kindness and love, and that they often take place in the simplest of forms. After all, we are each vulnerable, afraid, and imperfect but we are each also always worthy of love and belonging.

Our discussion opened Nicholas's eyes to the following:
- Giving up his room for his grandmother when she was staying with us during her cancer operation and treatment (while he slept on the air mattress)
- When friends have birthdays, he is always excited to buy them toys that they cannot buy (the intentions of his heart, is always in the right place)

- When he donated over 250 books for his school library because they were need for new books for kids. (he did this twice in two different schools)
- When he sees me sick and he steps up to wash the dishes for me and help with cleaning
- When his little cousins are visiting his grand-mother's house and he feels like the big brother reading to them, entertaining and chasing around looking after them
- When he gives his lunch to kids in school because they like what he had, and he comes home hungry at the end of the day
- The daily prayers for his family members to get well, get a job, or asking for good health etc.

When I pointed these out, his face lit up and started to feel better. He was so hard on himself about this and feeling that he did not contribute to ease the pain for others around him.

I tried to tell him the lesson here is about the human condition & the intentions of your heart. Generosity is about giving without expecting anything in return. The act of kindness is not measured by how grand or small they are.

It's about giving from the heart and coming to the aid of others, even if that means just listening to their hurt without judgment.

It's about being there for a friend that needs a shoulder to cry on and giving the gift of your time to hear and uplift someone who is down. In-turn, these simple gestures will actually help you grow spiritually.

To that end, I have learned my own lesson having this discussion with my son. That same day when I was feeling down and hard on myself, I realized that if am going to comfort my own son, I better believe in those same words that had come out of my mouth earlier.

Life will continue to challenge us whether personally or professionally. The key is not to let it take us down, but rather learn from those experiences along the way. It is equally important for us to remind ourselves as well about the good we do and that we are worthy as well.

As a good friend of my mine use to say, "people teach you how to treat them", noting that you need to not miss those lessons when they happen to you.

Some Advice

So, I say this to all the new EAs out there. As an Executive Assistant, you are in a role that comes from a place of service where you do the little things and the big things. Some of those days, the things you do will get noticed and oftentimes it won't.

You must decide how you will measure your own accomplishments; how you feel about yourself and your contributions, versus waiting on others to validate your efforts.

Small FYI, you will end up waiting a long time for that, as you can't change people's behaviors or actions, but you are definitely in control of how you react to them.

Keep reminding yourself that what you do is a support role with qualities and traits which stem from a place of service, care, intuition & excellence. It's a mind-set after-all. Either you have it or you don't and if you struggle with it, that means you are in the wrong profession.

If you choose to be thoughtful in your actions and support for others, the one thing I have learned is that the action of 'doing' is rewarding to me.

As evidence for me, thoughtfulness fills my cup every time, it doesn't cost much so I am a firm believer in doing with thoughtfulness!

As we make our way through life, it is important to give thanks to God and to those who have supported us and given us opportunity to grow.

Dear Reader,

Thank you for choosing to read my book out of the thousands available to choose from.

Reading a book takes time and quietness, so I am grateful that you have dedicated time to this enriching experience, whatever the book's title and subject.

Thanks to our ability to share our stories, we are able to see other lives that offer a window into their world in order to learn, grow and share in their experience.

I truly hope that what I have shared in my book, brings a message of hope, healing or helps in any way possible.

That's why I'm grateful that you chose to read my book.

If you have a moment, I encourage you to explore my Facebook page and Website (noted on the following page).

With profound gratitude and appreciation,

Amal

Volume #1 Collection
Author: Amal Candido

Thank you very much for your time to share in my experiences, hoping they will help you as well.

Talk soon when Volume 2 comes out. Until then, please drop by any of the spots online listed below:

Website: MyEABlog.com

Facebook: www.facebook.com/myEAblog/

Twitter: @myEAblogdotcom

Instagram: @myEABlog

www.ingramcontent.com/pod-product-compliance
Lightning Source LLC
Chambersburg PA
CBHW031426210526
45464CB00005B/2070